Amazing Cities

A Coloring Book of Fantastic Places in the World! Vol. 2

Artwork by Katia Petrunina & Viktoriya

GETTING STARTED

Bring out your imagination, arouse your senses and creativity, and as you become engaged in the pleasurable, soothing activity of Coloring, it calms you and instantaneously starts reducing your stress level.

We bring to you Vol. 2 of Amazing Cities This unique coloring book for grown-ups features immersive views of real cities from around the world. Inside you will find More than 35 fun activities that will take you on an artistic adventure to the fantastic places of the World.

This Freehand drawing with liner pen on paper, beautifully rendered and detailed line, from our favorite artist, shows visually arresting global locales from Vilnius in Lithuania, Saint Petersburg in Russia, and Padua in Italy to Strasbourg in France, Jerusalem in Israel, Melaka in Malaysia and Many More.

The adult coloring book's distinctive large square format offers absorbingly complex vistas to color, the crisp white pages are conducive to a range of artistic applications. Printed on high quality extra-thick paper, this inspiring coloring book for grownups is perfect for decorating with markers, colored pencils, gel pens, or watercolors. Printed on one side of the page to avoid bleed-through help keeps all the artwork fully colorable.

So take your time, relax, and let your imagination run free! Get out your markers or pens and discover the calming pleasure of coloring.

Safe travels!

JERUSALEM

ISRAEL

WARSAW

POLAND

VENICE

ITALY

STOCKERAU

AUSTRIA

BOHEMIAN CRUMLAW

CZECH REPUBLIC

JERUSALEM
ISRAEL

AKKO

ISRAEL

JERUSALEM

ISRAEL

VILNIUS

LITHUANIA

WARSAW

POLAND

SOSPEL

FRANCE

PALERMO

ITALY

PALERMO

ITALY

PALERMO
ITALY

TRIESTE
ITALY

VENICE

ITALY

CATANIA

ITALY

SAINT PETERSBURG

RUSSIA

PADUA

ITALY

VENICE

ITALY

MELAKA

MALAYSIA

DIU

INDIA

KUALA LUMPUR

MALAYSIA

Kuala Lumpur.

GEORGETOWN

MALAYSIA

MAE HONG SON

THAILAND

CHIANG MAI

THAILAND

VENICE

ITALY

SOSPEL

FRANCE

HUE
VIETNAM

HUE

VIETNAM

BONUS
Coloring Pages

Thank You

If you enjoyed Coloring the Amazing Cities in this book, please take a little time to share your thoughts and post a positive review with 5 star rating on Amazon, it would encourage me and make me serve you better. It'd Really be greatly appreciated.

We'll never be perfect, but that won't stop us from trying. Your feedback makes us serve you better. Send ideas, criticism, Compliment or anything else you think we should hear to info@adultscoloringartist.com. We'll Reply you As soon as we receive your Mail. :)

Visit our Author Page to get More Amazing Adults Coloring Books HERE>> https://www.amazon.com/author/adultcoloringbooksbestsellers

22864705R00049

Made in the USA
San Bernardino, CA
25 July 2015